1

CW00375699

MILOŠ SOVA

traveller's CZECH

collets

CONTENTS

MLUVÍTE ČESKY?

Mluvíte česky?	*mlooveeteh chesski*	Do you speak Czech?
Já nerozumím...	*yāh nehrozoomeem*	I don't understand...

You will often hear this whenever you venture on anything more than Čedok-guided trips and de luxe restaurants and hotels. This booklet should help you to overcome the feeling of bewilderment likely to seize you when you do not understand a single word of the language spoken around you. It does not claim to be a textbook of, or even an introduction to, the Czech language with its grammatical complications. For this, a proper language course would be necessary.

The present booklet is above all a **phrase-book** catering for strictly practical needs.

HINTS FOR USERS

1. Pronunciation is indicated throughout the book (with the exception of the Appendix), but you should go first through the remarks on Czech pronunciation (pp. 7, 8).

2. Look up your topic among the pictured symbols inside the cover page. There is also an alphabetic Index at the end of the book which allows of easy reference.

3. On the left you will find the most useful phrases, questions and answers. On the right-hand side opposite, the lexical material is arranged in alphabetic order, and you will also find there some of the most common notices and inscriptions.

4. Questions and answers you are likely to hear from a Czech are marked with an asterisk.

5. You will probably take up the subjects in the logical order in which they are presented, i. e. beginning with your arrival in Czechoslovakia. But the "rule of thumb" method may be used as well, and in case of necessity a Czech phrase may be pointed out to your Czech or Slovak informant.

6. The factual information given with the different topics is general in character and scope and cannot substitute a guide-book. For detailed information you should contact Čedok (see p. 20), which has offices in London, New York and many major European cities. L. Mot'ka's **Touring Czechoslovakia** contains reliable information on Czechoslovak Hotels and Restaurants.

CZECH WORDS

Whereas many French and German words are clearly recognizable to the English or American speaker, Czech and Slovak[1] words sound strange to your ears, with the exception, perhaps, of such words as **bratr** (brother), **sestra** (sister), **syn** (son), **tři** (three). You may also identify **víno** (wine), **mléko** (milk) and **husa** (goose). Many analogies, would however, be misleading: **ten den** (that day) has nothing to do with the number ten and a slum or a hovel! **Být či nebýt** (pron. *beet chee nehbeet*) is Hamlet's old question whether "to be or not to be" and has nothing in common with the extremely popular "big beat". A **dům** (pron. *doom*) means "house" and should not remind you of "Doomsday".

Some Czech words have been taken directly from English: **kempink** (camping), **sport, bar, fotbal, hokej** (hockey) and even **trable** (troubles). Many belong to the international wordstock, especially the scientific terms: **fyzika, matematika, foto, kino, auto** (pron. *owtôh* – *ow* as in how, now), **telegraf, telefon, pošta** (pron. *poshtah*, the post-office), **piano** (pron. *pee-āh-noh*), etc.

Before proceeding any further in our exploration of Czech words let us give you a brief description of the elements they consist of.

---

[1] Slovak is closely related to Czech. Broadcasts in Czech and Slovak are perfectly understood by the listeners of both nations.

Looking at the signs on shopfronts, at the inscriptions and notices in the streets, you will easily recognize the international words mentioned above. Piano and telefon give you the clue to the pronunciation of the Czech vowels. They are "pure", like the Italian vowels:

a   *ah*, pronounced approximately as in dull, some. Long **á** *āh* as in father, rather.

e   *eh*, as in bed, men (never as in me, he). Long **é** *ēh* is also transliterated as *air*, e. g. **malé** is pronounced *mullair*.

i   *i*, as in sit, bit. Long **í** is pronounced *ee* as in see, beet.

o   *oh*, as in hot, pot in English, not American, pronunciation. Long **ó** as in lord, sport.

u   *oo*, as in good, put. Long **ú** as in doom, rule.

y   sounds like *i*, that is, a short English *ee*. We transliterate it *y* (as in truly, study).

What about the many "accents", the symbols above the letters? What looks like an "accent" is in fact a mark of length: **káva** (coffee) is pronounced *kāh-vah* – the first **á** is long, the second **a** is short. We have therefore the series **a – á, e – é, i – í, o – ó, u – ú (or ů)**[1]**, y – ý.**

It is always the FIRST syllable of a word that is stressed in Czech. It must be pointed out at once that the stress **does not** lengthen a short vowel and that all vowels, in stressed and unstressed syllables, long or short, are **fully** pronounced. There is no reduction of the vowel sound in unstressed syllables as in English: **káva** must be pronounced with both **a**'s equally "clear", not *kāh-va* with the second **a** as in sofa.

Czech consonants often appear in clusters, such as **Brno** *bernoh*, **Vltava** *veltah-vah*, **zmrzlina** *zmurz-lee-nah*, ice-cream.

You will find below a synopsis of Czech consonants; only those differing from the English consonants are listed:

---

[1] The circle is used instead of the length-mark when long **u** appears in the middle or at the end of a word.

c	*ts* as in hats, cats. Ex. **Co?** *tsoh,* what? **Cena** *tsennah* price.
č	*ch* in church or *tch* in catch. Ex. **Čedok** *cheddock;* **čokoláda** *chockollahdah,* chocolate. You can see that the other "accent", the sign ˅ distinguishes **c** *ts* from **č** *ch* – co: **čokoláda.**
j	*yeh.* **Jeden** *yedden,* one. Both **e** s are equally clear!
s	*ss.* **Maso** *mussoh,* meat. Short **a**, short **o**; -*ss*-, not -*z*-.
š	*sh.* **Pošta** *poshtah,* post-office.
ž	*zh* as in pleasure, measure. Ex. **služba** *sloozhbah,* service.
ř	*zh* (approximately): **Dvořák.** This particular sound has an acoustic effect similar to what you hear in English words such as try, dry, tree. It does not exist in Slovak. You will be understood if you pronounce simply *dvorāk* or *dvozhāk.*
ch	is the sound you hear in the Scottish Loch-ness. We transliterate it by *kh.*
ď, ť, ň	are soft sounds you can hear in dew, tune, onion. Ex. **neděle** *neddyelleh,* Sunday. **Tisíc** *tyisseets,* thousand.
ě	is pronounced *yeh.* Ex. **oběd** *obyet,* lunch.
aj	*ai* resembles the English sound in fight, strike.
ej	*ei* as in day, great; **au** *aoo* as in how, now, out.
oj	*oi* as in boy, oyster; **ou** *ow* as in low, boat.

This is all you have to know about Czech sounds. The only accurate means of rendering them in print would be the script of the International Phonetic Association. For various reasons we have been obliged to adopt as a makeshift a more simple method, the **Imitated Pronunciation,** which will do quite well for our purpose, however inconsistent and fanciful it may be.

| Good morning | **Dobrý den** | *dobree den* |
| Good afternoon | **Dobré odpoledne** | *dobbreh otpolledneh* |

You can say **dobrý den** regardless of the time of the day.

In the morning you might also say	**dobré jitro**	*dobrěh yeetroh.*
Good evening	**Dobrý večer**	*dobree vecherr*
Good night	**Dobrou noc**	*dobrow nots*
Good bye	**Na shledanou**	*nah-skhleddunnow*
Thanks (thank you)	**Děkuji**	*dyekoo-yi*

The reply to this is: **prosím** *prosseem* not at all. Other uses of **prosím**:

please...; **prosím vás** *prosseem vahss* be kind enough to...
Prosím? (with rising intonation) I beg your pardon?
(What did you say? Please repeat it.)

| Yes – no | **Ano - ne** | *unnoh – neh* |
| Perhaps, maybe | **Snad, možná** | *snut, mozhnáh* |

Certainly	Jistě	yeestyeh
Where—is…?	Kde je…?	gdeh yeh
* Here – there	* Tady - tam	tuddy – tahm
Is it far?	Je to daleko?	yeh toh dullekkoh
* No, it's near.	* Ne, to je blízko.	neh, toh yeh bleeskoh
How far is it?	Jak je to daleko?	yuck yeh toh dullekkoh
When is lunch?	Kdy je oběd?	gdy yeh obyet
* It is ready.	* Je hotov.	yeh hottoff
* It isn't ready yet.	* Ještě není hotov.	yeshtyeh nennyee hottoff
How much does it cost?	Kolik to stojí?	kollick toh stoyee
What is the Czech for…?	Jak se řekne česky…?	yuck seh zhekneh chesski

1 **jeden** *yedden* – masculine   **jeden den** one day
   jedna *yednah* – feminine   **jedna káva**
                                        one coffee
   jedno *yednoh* – neuter   **jedno pivo**
                                        one beer

2 **dva** *dvah* – masc.   **dva dny** two days
   dvě *dvyeh* – femin. **dvě noci** *dvyeh notsi*
                              two nights

3 **tři** *tzhee*
4 **čtyři** *shteezhee*
5 **pět** *pyet*
6 **šest** *shest*
7 **sedm** *seddoom*
8 **osm** *ossoom*
9 **devět** *devvyet*
10 **deset** *desset*
11 **jedenáct** *yeddenáhtst*
12 **dvanáct** *dvunnáhtst*
13 **třináct** *tzheenáhtst*
14 **čtrnáct** *shternáhtst*
15 **patnáct** *puttnáhtst*
16 **šestnáct** *shestnáhtst*
17 **sedmnáct** *seddoomnáhtst*
18 **osmnáct** *ossoomnáhtst*

19	**devatenáct**	*devvuttehnăhtst*
20	**dvacet**	*dvutset*
21	**dvacet jeden,**	*dvutset yedden,* etc.
	or **jeden a dvacet**	*yedden ah dvutset*
22	**dvacet dva**	*dvutset dvah*
30	**třicet**	*tzhitset*
40	**čtyřicet**	*shteezhitset*
50	**padesát**	*puddessăht*
60	**šedesát**	*sheddessăht*
70	**sedmdesát**	*seddoomdessăht*
80	**osmdesát**	*ossoomdessăht*
90	**devadesát**	*devvuddessăht*
100	**sto** *stoh*	or: **jedno sto**
200	**dvě stě**	*dvyeh styeh*
300	**tři sta**	*tzhee stah*
400	**čtyři sta**	*shteeree stah*
500	**pět set**	*pyet set*
600	**šest set**	*shest set*
700	**sedm set**	*seddoom set*
800	**osm set**	*ossoom set*
900	**devět set**	*devvyet set*
1000	**tisíc**	*tyisseets*
2000	**dva tisíce**	*dvah tyisseetseh*
5000	**pět tisíc**	*pyet tyisseets*

Sunday	**neděle**	*neddyelleh*
Monday	**pondělí**	*pondyellee*
Tuesday	**úterý**	*ooteree*
Wednesday	**středa**	*stzheddah*
Thursday	**čtvrtek**	*shtvertek*
Friday	**pátek**	*păhtek*
Saturday	**sobota**	*sobbottah*
Speak slowly!	**Mluvte pomalu!**	*mloofteh pohmahloo*
Do you speak English?	**Mluvíte anglicky?**	*mlooveeteh anglitskee*
* No, I don't.	* **Ne, nemluvím.**	*neh nemlooveem*
Do you understand me?	**Rozumíte mi?**	*rozoomeeteh mee*
Tell me...	**Řekněte mi...**	*zheknyehteh mee*
* A little.	* **Trochu.**	*trockhoo*
Allow me...	**Dovolte...**	*dovvolteh*
Excuse me...	**Promiňte...**	*prohminteh*

11

(To this, you reply: **to nic** *toh nits*, or: **nic se nestalo** *nits seh nestulloh* that's nothing. You may also say: it's perfectly all right **to je v pořádku** *toh yeh fpozhátkoo*).

Sorry... but...	**Lituji... ale...**	*littooyi... ulleh...*
* Never mind.	* **To nevadí.**	*toh nevvuddyee*
I am glad.	**Jsem rád.**	*sem rāht*
* Are you English?	* **Jste Angličan?**	*steh unglitchun*
Yes, I am.	**Ano, jsem.**	*unnoh sem*
Listen! (Look here!)	**Poslyšte!**	*posslishteh*
Give me...	**Dejte mi...**	*dayteh mee*
Have you...?	**Máte...?**	*māhteh*
I like it.	**To se mi líbí.**	*tossemmee leebee*
* Come in!	* **Dále!**	*dāhleh*
	or **Vstupte!**	*fstoopteh*
* Sit down!	* **Sedněte si!**	*sednyetteh see*
* Wait!	* **Počkejte!**	*pochkayteh*
* Wait here	* **Počkejte zde (tady)**	*pochkayteh zdeh (tuddy)*
* Wait a minute	* **Počkejte moment**	*pochkayteh momment*
How long shall I wait?	**Jak dlouho budu čekat?**	*yuck dlowhoh boodoo checkutt*
* Five minutes.	* **Pět minut.**	*pyet minnoot*
* I don't know.	* **Nevím.**	*nevveem*
first	**první**	*pervnee*
second	**druhý**	*droohee*
third	**třetí**	*tzhettee*
fourth	**čtvrtý**	*shtvertee*
fifth	**pátý**	*pāhtee*
sixth	**šestý**	*shestee*
seventh	**sedmý**	*sedmee*
eight	**osmý**	*ossmee*
ninth	**devátý**	*devvāhtee*
tenth	**desátý**	*dessāhtee*
minute	**minuta** *f.*	*minnootah*
hour	**hodina** *f.*	*hoddyinnah*
half	**půl** *f.*	*pool*

quarter	**čtvrt** *f.*	*shtvert*	
day	**den** *m.*	*den*	
week	**týden** *m.*	*teeden*	
month	**měsíc** *m.*	*mnyesseets*	
year	**rok** *m.*	*rock*	

January	**leden** *m.*	*ledden*
February	**únor** *m.*	*oonor*
March	**březen** *m.*	*bzhezzen*
April	**duben** *m.*	*dooben*
May	**květen** *m.*	*kvyetten*
June	**červen** *m.*	*cherrven*
July	**červenec** *m.*	*cherrvennets*
August	**srpen** *m.*	*serrpen*
September	**září** *n.*	*zāhzhee*
October	**říjen** *m.*	*zhee-yen*
November	**listopad** *m.*	*listohputt*
December	**prosinec** *m.*	*prossinets*

"Small words" (to be learnt carefully):

kde? *gdeh* where? – **tady** or **zde** here – **tam** there
nahoře *nahozheh* upstairs – **dole** *dolleh* downstairs
napravo *nupprahvoh* to the right
nalevo *nullehvoh* to the left

kdy? *gdy* when? – **teď** *tet'* (ť is pronounced as in tune) now
potom *pottom* then, later
hned *hnet* at once, right away
už *oosh* already; **ještě ne** *yeshtye neh* not yet
ráno in the morning; **dopoledne** before noon
v poledne at noon; **odpoledne** afternoon
večer in the evening; **v noci** at night
v jednu hodinu at one o'clock
za hodinu in an hour
za chvíli *zak-khveely* in a moment
včera *fcherrah* yesterday
dnes today
zítra *zeetrah* tomorrow
tento týden this week
minulý týden last week

Introducing people

I am	**Jsem...** or:	*sem*
My name is ...	**Jmenuji se...**	*mennooyi seh*
and this is ...	**a to je...**	*ah toh yeh*
my wife	**má žena**	*māh zhennah*
my son	**můj syn**	*mooy sin*
my daughter	**má dcera**	*māh tserrah*
I am very glad	**Jsem velmi rád,**	*sem velmee rāht*
to meet you.	**že vás**	*zheh vāhss*
	poznávám.	*poznāhvāhm*
	Or: **Těší mě.**	*tyeshee mnyeh*

Introduce me,	**Představte mě**	*pzhet-stufteh mnyeh*
please, to Mr...	**laskavě panu...**	*luskuvyeh punnoo*
to Mrs...	**paní...**	*punnyee*
to Miss...	**slečně...**	*slechnyeh*
* With pleasure	* **S radostí**	*sruddostyee*

Apologies, expressions of regret, etc.

I hope you will excuse me.	**Doufám, že mi prominete.**	*dowfāhm zheh mee prohminnetteh*
I must apologize.	**Musím se vám omluvit.**	*moosseem seh vāhm omloovit*
* It doesn't matter. * Never mind.	* **To nevadí**	*toh nevvuddyee*
Pardon me!	**Odpusťte!**	*otpoosteh*

Expressions of assent and dissent

Of course	**ovšem**	*ofshem*
That's true	**to je pravda**	*to yeh prahvdah*
It is so	**je to tak**	*yeh toh tuk*
Not at all	**vůbec ne**	*voobets neh*
That's not true	**to není pravda**	*toh nehnyee prahvdah*
You are mistaken	**mýlíte se**	*meeleeteh seh*
I hope so	**doufám, že ano**	*dowfāhm zhe unnoh*
I agree	**souhlasím**	*sowhlusseem*
That will do	**to stačí**	*toh stutchee*
I don't think so	**Myslím, že ne**	*meesleem zheh neh*
Perhaps yes	**asi ano**	*ussi unnon*
That's not enough	**to nestačí**	*toh nehstahtchee*

Various questions   and answers

How are you? **Jak se máte?**
yuck seh māteh

Děkuji, mám se dobře.
dyehooyi māhm seh dobzheh
Thanks, I am well

What's the matter with you?
Co je vám? *tsoh yeh vāhm*

Nic mi není *nits mee nennyee* There is nothing the matter with me.

* Have you... any children?
* **Máte... děti** *dyetyi*

* **Ano, mám.** Yes, I have.
* **Ne, nemám.** No, I have not.

* Are you married? **Jste ženatý?** *steh zhennuttee*
(asking a woman): * **Jste vdaná?** *steh vdunnāh*

   * **Ano, jsem** *unnoh sem*
* **Ne, nejsem** *neh naysem*
* **Ne, jsem svobodná** *sem svobbodnāh* I am unmarried

* Have you * **Máte čas?**
any time to spare? *māhteh chuss*

* **Teď** *teť* **nemám čas, až zítra** *ush zeetrah* – only tomorrow

15

Where are you from?	* Od-	* Jsem z Prahy, z Londýna
kud jste? *otkoot steh*		*sem sprah-hy zlondeenah*
Do you like...?	Máte rád	*māhteh rāht*
	(a woman: ráda)?	*(rāhdah)*

Various requests (in addition to those already met with, such as: **dejte mi, řekněte mi, počkejte, sedněte si,** etc., see p. 12).

Come here!	Pojďte sem!	*pot-teh sem*
Go home!	Jděte domů!	*dyetteh dommoo*
Stop!	Zastavte!	*zustufteh*
Go on driving!	Jeďte dál!	*yet-teh dāhl*
Call him!	Zavolejte ho!	*zuvvolayteh hoh*
Repeat it!	Opakujte to!	*oppuckoo-yteh toh*
Ring him up!	Zatelefonujte mu!	*zuttelleh-fonnooyteh moo*
Stay here!	Zůstaňte zde!	*zoostunn-teh zdeh*
Open it!	otevřte!	*otevv-zhteh*
Shut it!	zavřete!	*zuvv-zhetteh*
Come and see us!	Přijďte k nám!	*pzhit-teh knāhm*
Push – pull	tam – sem	
(the swing-door)	(k sobě)	*k sobbyeh*
Write it!	Napište to!	*nuppishteh toh*
Read it!	Přečtěte to!	*pzhech-tyetteh toh*
Don't forget!	Nezapomeňte!	*Nehzuppohmenteh*
One moment,	Okamžik,	*okumzhik*
please!	prosím!	*prosseem*
Show it to me!	Ukažte mi to!	*ookushteh mee toh*
This way, please!	Tudy prosím!	*toody prossem*
Hurry up!	Pospěšte si!	*pospyeshteh see*

TRAVELLING

BY CAR

Which way is it to...?	**Kudy se jede do...?**	*koody seh yeddeh doh...*
* Drive straight on.	* **Jeďte rovně.**	*yet-teh rovnyeh*
* First turning to the left (right).	* **První ulice vlevo (vpravo).**	*pervnee oolitseh vlevvoh (fprăhvoh)*
Can you show me it on the map?	**Můžete mi to ukázat na mapě?**	*moozhehteh mee toh ookăhzutt năhmuppyeh*

Is this the right way to...?	**Jedu dobře do...?**	*yeddoo dobzheh doh...*
* No, you must go back to the crossing.	* **Ne, musíte se vrátit na křižovatku.**	*neh mooseeteh seh vrăhtit nah kzhizhovvutkoo*
* You mustn't drive here.	* **Tudy nesmíte jet.**	*toody nehsmeeteh yet*

It's closed to traffic.	**Cesta je uzavřena.**	*tsestah yeh oozăhvzhennah*
Where is the nearest petrol-station? (gas station)	**Kde je nejbližší čerpací stanice?**	*gdeh yeh nayblishee cherrputsee stunnitseh*
Over there, at the corner.	**Tamhle, na rohu.**	*tăhm-hleh nah-ro-hoo*
Have you got high-grade petrol? (gas)	**Máte speciál?**	*măhteh spetsi-ăhl*
Give me 10 litres.	**Dejte mi deset litrů.**	*dayteh mee desset litroo*
Is it allowed to camp here?	**Je dovoleno tady tábořit?**	*yeh dovvollennoh tuddy tăhbozhit*
It is forbidden.	**To je zakázáno.**	*toh yeh zahkăhzăh-noh*
What is the name of this (village, town, street, square)?	**Jak se jmenuje (ta vesnice, to město, ta ulice, to náměstí)?**	*yuck seh mennoo-yeh (tah vesnitseh, toh mnyestoh, tah oolitseh, toh năhmyestyee*
Is there a car-repair shop here?	**Je zde autoopravna?**	*yeh zdeh aootoh-opruvnah*
accident	**úraz** m.	*ooruss*
battery	**baterie** f.	*buttaireeyeh*
bicycle	**kolo** n.	*kolloh*
brake	**brzda** f.	*berzdah*
bus	**autobus** m.	*aootohbooss*
camping site	**autokemp** m.	*aootohkemp*
can	**kanistr** m.	*kunnisterr*
car	**vůz** m.	*vooss*
chain	**řetěz** m.	*zhettyess*
door	**dveře**	*dvehzheh*
to drive	**řídit**	*zheedyit*
driver	**řidič** m.	*zhidditch*
driving licence	**řidičský průkaz** m.	*zhidditchskee proockas*
engine	**motor** m.	*mottorr*
exhaust	**výfuk** m.	*veefook*
frontier	**hranice** f.	*hrunnitseh*
frontier crossing	**hraniční přechod** m.	*hrunnitchnyee pzhekhott*

to grease	(na)mazat	(nah)mahzutt
high road	silnice f.	silnitseh
to hire	najmout	nighmowt
to hoot	troubit	trowbit
(to blow one's horn)		
mountain	hora f.	horrah
petrol (gas)	benzín m.	benzeen
radiator	chladič m.	khludditch
a repair	oprava f.	oprahvah
to repair	opravit	oprahvit
right of way	přednost v jízdě	pzhednost vyeezdyeh
scenery	krajina	krah-yinnah
screw (bolt)	šroub m.	shrowp
to slow down	zpomalit	spomullit
slowly	pomalu	pohmahloo
spare	náhradní	näh-hrudnyee
parts	součástky f.	sowchähstky
speed	rychlost f.	rikhlost
to speed up	zrychlit	zrikhlit
spring	pero n.	perroh
spring	pružina f.	proozhinnah
steering wheel	volant m.	vollunt
to switch on	zapnout	zupnowt
to switch off	vypnout	vipnowt
tank	nádrž	nähderzh
traffic	doprava f.	dopravah
traffic regulations	dopravní předpisy	doprahvnyee pzhetpissy
traffic lights	dopravní světla n.	doprahvnyee svyetlah
turning	zatáčka f.	zuttäh-chkah
tyre (tire)	pneumatika f.	pneoo-muttickah
valley	údolí n.	oodollee
valve	ventil m.	ventil
to wash	(u)mýt	(oo)meet
wheel	kolo n.	kollōh
wood	les m.	less
petrol pump (gas station)	benzinová pumpa	benzeenohväh poompah
rope	lano n.	lunnōh

JEĎTE POMALU	Drive Slowly
NÁLEDÍ	Road Ice-bound
JEDNOSMĚRNÁ ULICE	One-way Street
OTEVŘENO	Open
PARKOVÁNÍ ZAKÁZÁNO	No Parking
PITNÁ VODA	Drinking-Water
POZOR!	Caution!
PRŮJEZD ZAKÁZÁN	No Thoroughfare
NECHRÁNĚNÝ PŘEJEZD	Level Crossing
OBJÍŽĎKA	Diversion (Detour)
VJEZD	Entrance
VÝJEZD	Exit
UZAVŘENO	Closed to Traffic
ZÁKAZ STÁNÍ	No Waiting
ŽIVOTU NEBEZPEČNO	Danger
ŽÁDNÝ VÝCHOD	No Exit

● For all information concerning motoring you should apply to Autoturist, Praha 1, Opletalova 29, tel. 22-35-44, and to the Czechoslovak Travel Bureau ČEDOK, Praha 1 Na příkopě 18, tel. 22-34-20 or 22-42-51. You will see in the hall there a large-scale map of Prague and its outskirts with the main traffic routes clearly indicated.

All alcoholic drinks are strictly prohibited for car drivers!

If you have an engine trouble the following phrases may be useful:

The engine is stalling	**Motor vynechává**	*mottorr vinnehkhāhvāh*
The engine won't start	**Motor nezabírá**	*mottorr nehzubbeerāh*
* We must:	*** Musíme:**	*moosseemeh*
clean	**vyčistit**	*vitchistit*
(change)	**(vyměnit)**	*(vimnyenit)*

English	Czech	Pronunciation
spark plugs	svíčky	sveechky
check	zkontrolovat	skontrollovutt
the ignition	zapalování n.	zahpahlovvähnee
blow up	napumpovat	nahpoompohvutt
the tyres (the tires)	pneumatiky f.	pneoomutticky
Can you give me a lift?	Můžete mě svézt?	moozhehteh mnye svairst
* With pleasure.	* S radostí.	sruddostee
Can you give me a hand?	Můžete mi pomoci?	moozhehteh mee pomotsi
I have had a puncture (a flat tire)	Praskla mi pneumatika.	prahsklah mee pneoomuttickah

BY TRAIN AND BY AIR

English	Czech	Pronunciation
Two first-class tickets for...	Dva lístky první třídy do...	dvah leestky pervnyee tzheedy doh
Which platform?	Které nástupiště?	ktehrair nähstoopishtyeh
* Third platform	* Třetí nástupiště	tzhettyee nähstoopishtyeh
* Second track	* Druhá kolej	droo-hāh kollay
Is there a dining-car on the train?	Je ve vlaku jídelní vůz?	yeh vehvlahkoo yeedelnee vooss
Is this a through train?	Je to přímý vlak?	yeh toh pzheemee vluck
* You must change at...	* Musíte přestoupit v...	moosseeteh pzhestowpit v...
When does the train to... leave?	Kdy odjíždí vlak do...?	gdy odyeezhdee vluck doh...
When does it arrive in Prague?	Kdy přijede do Prahy?	gdy pzhi-yeddeh dohpra-hy
* It is overdue.	* Má zpoždění.	mäh spozh-dyenee
Is this seat free?	Je to místo volné?	Yeh toh meestoh volnair
* No, it's taken.	* Ne, je obsazeno.	neh, yeh opsuzzennoh

21

English	Czech	Pronunciation
Excuse me, this is my seat.	Promiňte, to je moje místo.	prohminnteh, toh yeh moyeh meestoh
I made a reservation.	Mám místenku.	māhm meestenkoo
How long does the train stop in this station?	Jak dlouho stojí vlak v této stanici?	yuck dlowhoh stoyee vluck ftairtoh stahnitsi
Shall I close the window (the door)?	Mám zavřít okno (dveře)?	māhm zuvv-zheet oknoh (dvehzheh)
It's draughty in here.	Tady táhne.	tuddy tāh-hneh
* As you like	* Jak si přejete	yuck see pzheh-yetteh
* What do you want?	* Co si přejete?	tso see pzheh-yetteh
I need a transit visa.	Potřebuji průjezdní vízum.	potzhebbooyi proo-yezdnee veezoom
I want a taxi.	Chci taxi.	kh-tsee tuxi
* Do you want to go to the hotel or to the station?	* Chcete jet do hotelu nebo na nádraží?	kh-tsetteh yet doh hottelloo nebboh nah-nāhdrahzhee
When should I be at the airport?	Kdy mám být na letišti?	gdy māhm beet nah lettishti
Take this to the weighing-in desk.	Zaneste to k váze.	zunnesteh toh kvāh-zeh.

● Every year the Czechoslovak State Railways publish a Railway Guide containing all information (pp. 14–16, 54–55, in English) on trains, international passenger traffic, exchange-offices, etc.

English	Czech	Pronunciation
airport	letiště n.	lettishtye
airplane	letadlo n.	letuddloh
arrival	příjezd m.	pzhee-yest
(by air)	přílet m.	pzhee-let
bag	taška f.	tushkah
berth	lehátko n.	leh-hāhtkoh
booking-office	osobní pokladna f.	ossobnee pokluddnah

English	Czech	Pronunciation
carriage (wagon)	**vagón** *m.*	*vuggōhn*
compartment	**oddíl** *m.*	*oddyeel*
connection	**spojení** *n.*	*spo-yennee*
customs	**celnice** *f.*	*tselnitseh*
departure	**odjezd** *m.*	*odyest*
(by air)	**odlet** *m.*	
engine	**lokomotiva** *f.*	*lockomotteevah*
enquiries	**informace** *f.*	*inforrmahtseh*
(information)		
cloak-room	**šatna** *f.*	*shutnah*
cable railway	**lanovka** *f.*	*lunnofkah*
lavatory	**záchod** *m.*	*zāh-khot*
luggage	**zavazadla** *n.*	*zuvvah-zuddlah*
light luggage	**ruční**	*roochnyee*
	zavazadlo *n.*	*zuvvah-zuddloh*
left-luggage	**úschovna**	*ooskhovnah*
office (luggage room)	**zavazadel** *f.*	*zuvvah-zuddel*
station master	**přednosta**	*pzhednostah*
	stanice *m.*	*stunnitseh*
steamboat	**parník** *m.*	*parrn-eek*
a stop	**zastávka** *f.*	*zustāhfkah*
local train	**osobní vlak** *m.*	*ossobnee vluck*
suitcase	**kufřík** *m.*	*koofzheek*
porter	**nosič** *m.*	*nossitch*
rails	**koleje** *f.*	*kolleh-yeh*
railway	**dráha** *f.*	*drāh-hah*
railway fare	**jízdné** *n.*	*yeezdnair*
railway guide	**jízdní řád** *m.*	*yeezdnyee zhāht*
railway station	**nádraží** *n.*	*nāhdrahzhee*
return ticket	**zpáteční**	*spāh-tech-nyee*
	lístek *m.*	*leestek*
window-seat	**místo u okna** *n.*	*meestoh oo oknah*
extra charge	**doplatek** *m.*	*doplutteck*
guard	**průvodčí** *m.*	*proovot-chee*
(train conductor)		
sleeper	**lůžkový vůz** *m.*	*looshkovee vooss*
lorry (truck)	**nákladní auto** *n.*	*nāhkludnyee aootoh*
stop!	**stůjte!**	*stooyteh* or:
	zastavit!	*zustuvvit*
motor boat	**motorový**	*mottorrovee*
	člun	*chloon*

23

tag	štítek *m.*	*shteeteck*
through (coach, train)	přímý (vůz, vlak)	*pzheemee*
ticket	lístek *m.*	*leesteck*
	jízdenka *f.*	*yeezdenkah*
air ticket	letenka *f.*	*lettenkah*
time table	jízdní řád *m.*	*yeezdnyee zhaht*
trunk	kufr *m.*	*kooferr*

ČEKÁRNA	Waiting-room
MUŽI – ŽENY	Men – Women
VOLNO	Free
OBSAZENO	Engaged
NASTUPOVAT!	All aboard!
OBČERSTVENÍ	Refreshments
PODEJ ZAVAZADEL	Registration of Luggage
TEPLO	Warm
CHLADNO	Cold
KUŘÁCI	Smokers
NEKUŘÁCI	Non-s.
KOUŘENÍ ZAKÁZÁNO	No Smoking
MÍSTENKY	Reservations
VÝDEJ ZAVAZADEL	Delivery of Luggage
VSTUP ZAKÁZÁN	No Entry
ZÁCHRANNÁ BRZDA	Alarm Signal
ZTRÁTY A NÁLEZY	Lost Property Office

"Small words" (see p. 13):

Kudy?	*koody*	which way
Jak?	*yuck*	how?
Kolik?	*kollick*	how much, how many
Kam?	*kumm*	where to?
Odkud?	*otkoot*	where from?
Proč?	*protch*	why?

answers:

tudy	*toody*	this way
dobře	*dobzheh*	well
špatně	*shputtnyeh*	badly
moc	*mots*	much, a lot
málo	*mãhloh*	little

velmi	*velmee*	very
Do hotelu	*doh hottelluh*	to the hotel
Do Prahy	*doh prahhy*	to Prague
Z Anglie	*s angleeyeh*	from England
Z Ameriky	*ss Amerricki*	from America
Protože...	*prottoh-zheh*	because...
Kdo?	*gdoh*	who?
Co?	*tsoh*	what?
Kdo je to?	*gdoh yeh toh*	who is it?
Co je to?	*tsoh yeh toh*	What is this?

Personal pronouns:

já	*yah*	I	**my**	*mee*	we
on	*on*	he	**vy**[1]	*vee*	you[1]
ona	*onnah*	she	**oni**	*onnyi*	they

[1] (several people and polite address of one person)

"To Be":

já jsem	*yāh' sem*	I am
on je	*on yeh*	he is
ona je	*onnah yeh*	she is
my jsme	*mee smeh*	we are
vy jste	*vee steh*	you are
oni jsou	*onnyi sow*	they are

"To Have":

já mám	*yāh' māhm*	I have
on má	*on māh*	he has
ona má	*onnah māh*	she has
my máme	*mee māhmeh*	we have
vy máte	*vee māhteh*	you have
oni mají	*onnyi mah-yee*	they have

The 2nd person sing. – **ty,** thou – is only used to address little children, intimate friends and sometimes also professional colleagues.

Personal pronouns are usually left out with verbs: **máte** = **vy máte; jsme** = **my jsme.** Question: **máte?** have you? **Jste?** Are you?

Negation: **nemáme** *nemmāhmeh* we have not. **Ne-** is stressed; short *eh!* **Nejste** *naysteh* **pan Smith?** Aren't you Mr Smith? **Ne, nejsem** *neh naysem* No, I am not. **Jsem pan Black.** I am Mr. B.

Addressing people:

Female personal names (surnames) take the suffix **-ová:**

pan Novák Mr Novák   **paní Nováková**   Mrs Novak
                        slečna Nováková Miss Novak

Jak se máte *yuck seh māhteh* **pane doktore?** (liter. Mister Doctor)

How are you   **paní doktorko?** (Mrs Doctor)
                 slečno Černá? (Miss Black)

See also: Travelling

Please tell me the way to Wenceslas Square.	**Prosím, řekněte mi, jak se dostanu na Václavské náměstí.**	*prosseem zheknyeteh mee yuck seh dostunnoo nahvähts-lav-skair nähmnyestee*
Can I walk there?	**Můžu tam jít pěšky?**	*moozhoo tum yeet pyeshky*
* Take a taxi.	* **Jeďte taxíkem.**	*yet-teh tuxeekem*
Are you free?	**Jste volný?**	*steh volnee*
* No, I'm engaged.	* **Ne, jsem zadán.**	*neh sem zuddähn*
* Where do you want to go?	* **Kam chcete jet?**	*kum kh-tsetteh yet*
Take me to the Main Station	**Zavezte mě na Hlavní nádraží**	*zuvvesteh mnyeh nah-hluvnee näh-drah-zhee*
to the Castle	**na Hrad**	*nah hrut*
to Charles' bridge.	**ke Karlovu mostu.**	*keh karrlovvoo mostoo*
I want (I wish) to hire a car.	**Chci (přeju si) najmout vůz.**	*kh-tsee (pzheh-yoo-see) nighmowt vooss*
Is there a bus to...?	**Jede do ... autobus?**	*yeddeh doh... aoo-tobbooss*
* Yes, every ten minutes.	* **Ano, každých deset minut.**	*unnoh kuzhdeekh desset minnoot*
When will the next bus go?	**Kdy pojede příští autobus?**	*gdy poyeddeh pzhee-shtee aoo-tobbooss*
* In five minutes.	* **Za pět minut.**	*zuppyet minnoot*
Is this the right way to...?	**Jdu** (or: **jedu**) **dobře do...? (na...?)**	*ydoo (yeddoo) dobzheh doh... (nah...)*
Which tram (street car) shall I take?	**Kterou tramvají mám jet?**	*kterrow trum-vah-yee mahm yet*
* Change at the Museum to...	* **Přestupte u Musea na...**	*pzeh-stoopteh oo moozeh-ah nah...*

English	Czech	Pronunciation
* Any more fares?	* **Přistoupil někdo?**	*pzhee-stowpil nyegdoh*
* Move up to the front, please.	* **Postupte dále do vozu!**	*postoopteh dāhleh dovvozzoo*
avenue	**třída** *f.*	*tzheedah*
bridge	**most** *m.*	*most*
building	**budova** *f.*	*boodohvah*
castle	**hrad; zámek** *m.*	*zāhmek*
cemetery	**hřbitov** *m.*	*zhbittof*
church	**kostel** *m.*	*kostell*

district	**okres** *m.*	*okress*
embankment	**nábřeží** *n.*	*nāhbzheh-zhee*
factory	**továrna** *f.*	*tovvāhr-nah*
garden	**zahrada** *f.*	*zuhrah-dah*
to get on	**nastupovat**	*nustoo-povvutt*
to get off	**vystupovat**	*vee-stoo-povvutt*
hospital	**nemocnice** *f.*	*nehmots-nitseh*
house	**dům** *m.*	*doom*
market	**trh** *m.*	*terkh*
monument	**pomník** *m.*	*pomneek*
palace	**palác** *m.*	*pah-lāhts*
pavement (sidewalk)	**chodník** *m.*	*khodneek*
paving	**dlažba** *f.*	*dluzh-bah*
pedestrian	**pěší**	*pyeshee*
playground	**hřiště** *n.*	*h-zhee-shtyeh*
ramparts	**hradby** *f.*	*hruddby*
region	**kraj** *m.*	*cry*
river	**řeka** *f.*	*zhehkah*
road	**cesta** *f.*	*tsestah*
highway	**silnice** *f.*	*silnitseh*
super-highway	**dálnice** *f.*	*dāhlnitseh*
school	**škola** *f.*	*shkollah*
spa	**lázně** *n.*	*lāhz-nyeh*
spire	**věž** *f.*	*vyesh*
square	**náměstí** *n.*	*nāh-mnyestee*
statue	**socha** *f.*	*soh-khah*
suburb	**předměstí** *n.*	*przedmnyestee*
taxi-rank	**stanoviště** *n.*	*stunnovvishtyeh*
theatre	**divadlo** *n.*	*dyeevudloh*
tower	**věž** *f.*	*vyesh*
town-hall	**radnice** *f.*	*ruddnitseh*
tree	**strom** *m.*	*stromm*
works	**závod** *m.*	*zāhvot*

VSTUP	Way In
VÝSTUP	Way Out
PŘECHOD ZAKÁZÁN	No Crossing
ZASTÁVKA	Stop
POZOR NA SCHOD	Mind the Step
ČERSTVĚ NATŘENO	Wet Paint

● Taxi-service. – Prague taxis are marked with a broken white stripe and can be ordered by phone (24-25-41). You may also rent a car for shorter or longer trips outside of Prague, at PRAGOCAR Praha 1, Nové Město, Štěpánská 42 (next to the Hotel Alcron) – tel. 24-00-89, 24-84-85 or at the Prague Airport, tel. 334.

● Municipal transport system. – In trams, trolleybuses and buses you pay 1.— — 2.— Kčs, and you may change twice to other lines with one ticket. All the year round, Prague trams and buses are crowded between 5.30 and 7.30 a. m., and between 4 and 6.30 p. m.

● The historical core of Prague with its narrow streets and age-old monuments, and Charles bridge with its baroque statues, are closed to traffic.

● The capital of Czechoslovakia is steeped in history. A casual visitor to Prague is probably unaware that contacts between England and the ancient Kingdom of Bohemia go back to the Middle Ages. Professor J. V. Polišenský's "Britain and Czechoslovakia, a Study in Contacts" gives a lively account of all this.

Two important verbs:

jít   *yeet* to go on foot, to walk – **jet** *yet* to go by a vehicle, to travel.
Ex. **Kam jdete?** Where are you going? – **Jdu domů** I am going home. **Kam jedete?** Where are you travelling? – **Jedu (autem,** by car; **tramvají** by tram; **autobusem** by bus) **do města,** I am going to town.

Some prepositions:

do   to, into: **jdete do hotelu?** *detteh doh hottelloo.* Are you going to the hotel? **Ne, nejdu** *neh naydoo* No, I am not. **Jdu domů** *ydoo dohmoo* I am going home.

na: **Jedete na nádraží?** *yeddetteh nah-nāhdrazhee* Are you going to the station? (asking a driver). – **Ne, nejedu** *neh neh-yeddoo,* **jedu na letiště** *yeddoo nah lettishtyeh.* No, I am not, I am going (= driving a car) to the airport.

k, ke   to, towards: **ke Karlovu mostu; ke katedrále.**

AT A HOTEL

See also: Travelling, Getting about Town

Can you recommend me a good hotel?	Můžete mi doporučit dobrý hotel?	*moozhetteh mee doppohroochit dobree hottel*
I'd like a double bedroom with bath (without bath).	Chtěl bych pokoj s dvěma lůžky s koupelnou (bez koupelny).	*khtyel bikh pokoy zdvyemmah looshky skowpelnow (bess kowpelny)*
* Sorry, all rooms are booked.	* Lituji, všechny pokoje jsou zadány.	*littooyi fshekhny pockoyeh sow zuddǎhny*

* There is one single room left on the 5th floor.	* Jeden jednolůžkový pokoj je volný v pátém poschodí.	*yedden yednoh-looshkovvee pokoy yeh volnee fpǎhtehm po-skhoddyee*
Is there an elevator?	Je tam výtah?	*yeh tum veetakh*
* Yes, there is.	* Ano, je.	*unnoh yeh*
* (No, there is not)	* (Ne, není).	*neh nennyee*

English	Czech	Pronunciation
* Breakfast and service are charged separately.	* Snídaně a obsluha se platí zvlášt.	snyeedunnyeh ah opsloo-hah seh pluttee zvlähsht
I should like to see the manager.	Chtěl bych vidět pana vedoucího.	khtyel bikh viddyet punnah veddowtsee-hoh
I'll stay for one night only (for 3 days).	Zůstanu jen jednu noc (tři dny).	zoostunnoo yen yednoo nots (tzhee dny)
My luggage is at the station (in my car).	Moje zavazadla jsou na nádraží (ve voze).	moyeh zuvvah-zuddlah sow nah-nähdrahzhee (vevvozzeh)
Fetch it, please.	Přineste mi je laskavě.	pzhinnesteh mee yeh luskuvyeh
I'll leave tomorrow morning.	Odjedu zítra ráno.	odyedoo zeetrah räh-noh
Call me (wake me up) at 7 o'clock, please.	Vzbuďte mě v sedm hodin, prosím.	zboot-teh mnyeh fseddoom hoddin prosseem
Prepare the bill, please.	Připravte účet, prosím.	pzhipruvteh oochet prosseem
bath-room	koupelna f.	kowpelnah
bathtub	vana f.	vunnah
bed	postel f.	postell
	lůžko n.	looshkoh
bedroom	ložnice f.	lozhnitseh
bedclothes	ložní prádlo n.	lozhnyee präh-dloh
bell	zvonek m.	zvonnek
bill (check)	účet m.	oochet
blanket	pokrývka f.	pokreefkah
breakfast	snídaně f.	snyeedunnyeh
to have b.	snídat	snyeedutt
café	kavárna f.	kuvvähr-nah
camp	tábor m.	täh-borr
corridor	chodba f.	khod-bah
deposit	záloha f.	zäh-loh-hah
dining-room	jídelna f.	yeedelnah
doorman	vrátný m.	vräht-nee

floor	**poschodí** *n.*	*poskhoddyee*
guest	**host** *m.*	*host*
heating	**topení** *n.*	*toppennyee*
key	**klíč** *m.*	*kleetch*
lavatory	**toaleta** *f.*	*toallettah*
lounge	**hala** *f.*	*hullah*
manager	**vedoucí** *m. f.*	*veddowtsee*
operator	**telefonistka** *f.*	*tellefoh-nist-kah*
passport	**cestovní pas** *m.*	*tesestovnyee pass*
to pay	**platit**	*pluttit*
pub (bar)	**hospoda** *f.*	*hospoddah*
reception	**recepce** *f.*	*reh-tsep-tseh*
room	**pokoj** *m.*	*pockoy*
room-maid	**pokojská** *f.*	*pockoy-skāh*
service	**obsluha** *f.*	*opsloo-hah*
sheet	**prostěradlo** *n.*	*prostye-ruddloh*
shower	**sprcha** *f.*	*sper-khah*
sleeping bag	**spací pytel** *m.*	*sputsee pittel*
snack bar	**bufet** *m.*	*boofet*
soap	**mýdlo** *n.*	*meedloh*
storey (floor)	**patro** *n.*	*puttroh*
tent	**stan** *m.*	*stun*
tip	**spropitné** *n.*	*spropitnair*
towel	**ručník** *m.*	*rooch-nyeek*
twin-bed	**postel** *f.* **pro dva**	*postell pro dvah*
waiter	**číšník** *m.*	*cheesh-nyeek*
waitress	**číšnice** *f.*	*cheesh-nitseh*
wine cellar	**vinárna** *f.*	*vinnāhr-nah*
wash-basin	**umyvadlo** *n.*	*oomi-vuddloh*
youth hostel	**noclehárna** *f.*	*notsleh-ahrna*

VOLNÉ POKOJE	Rooms Free (Vacancy)
OBSAZENO	No Vacancies
POHOSTINSTVÍ	Inn
AUTOMAT	Buffet
PÁNI	Gentlemen
DÁMY	Ladies

● The hotels are divided into 6 categories (A-luxe, A', A, B', B and C) and graded in price according to the standard of amenities and services provided.

• For all information on accommodation (hotels, motels, motor camping sites, tent camps etc.) you should apply either to Čedok or to another Travel Agency: Rekrea, tel. 637-32; Balnea, tel. 646-77; Sport-Tourist 629-46; Youth Travel Bureau tel. 26-85-07. You may also ring up the Prague Information Service (Tel. 5-44444, Na příkopě 20, Praha 1) where you can buy city maps, "The Month in Prague", a very useful pamphlet, and other essential literature on Prague.

Some **prepositions** (continued from p. 30):

v, ve	in, at:	**v Praze** *fprah-zeh*, in P.; **v hotelu** *vhotelloo*
na	on, at:	**na letišti** *nah lettishti*, on the airfield
z, ze	out, of, from:	**z Prahy** *sprah-hy*, from P. Ex.★ **Jedete z Prahy?** Are you coming from Prague? **– Ano, jedu z Prahy do Brna.** Yes, I am leaving Prague for Brno
od	from:	**dopis od bratra,** a letter from my brother
u	at, near, by:	**bydlím u bratra,** I live at my brother's place
s, se	with:	**pokoj s koupelnou** a room with bath
bez	without:	**pokoj bez koupelny; čaj bez cukru** *tchai bess tsookroo* tea without sugar
před	before:	**před obědem,** before lunch
po	after:	**po večeři,** after dinner

AT A RESTAURANT

See also: At a Hotel

I need a table for	**Potřebuji stůl**	*potzhebbooyi stool*
... persons.	**pro ... osoby.**	*proh ... ossohby*
Waitress,	**Slečno, jídelní**	*slechnoh yeedelnyee*
the menu, please!	**lístek, prosím!**	*leestek prosseem*
Have you some	**Máte**	*mahteh*
national dish?	**nějaké**	*nyeh-yuckair*
	národní jídlo?	*nährodnee yeedloh*

Do you serve	**Máte "menu"**	*mähte "menny"*
regular dinners or	**nebo jenom jídla**	*nebboh yehnom*
only a la carte	**podle**	*yeedlah podleh*
meals?	**lístku?**	*leestkoo*
* What will you	* **Co budete pít?**	*tsoh boodetteh peet*
drink?		
I'd like a glass	**Chtěl bych**	*khtyel bikh*
of Pilsner.	**sklenici**	*sklennitsi*
	plzeňského.	*pelzenskair-hoh*

35

Give me two decilitres of red wine.	Dejte mi dvě deci červeného vína.	*dayteh mee dvyeh detsi chairvennair-hoh veenah*
I only want a snack.	Chci jenom něco malého.	*kh-tsee yennom nyetsoh mallair-hoh*
* Certainly, sir.	* K službám, pane.	*k'sloozhbähm punneh*
I don't eat meat.	Maso nejím.	*Mussoh neh-yeem*
I didn't order that dish.	To jídlo jsem neobjednal.	*toh yeedloh sem neh-obyednull*
Take it back.	Odneste to.	*Odnessteh toh*
I'd like black coffee and ice-cream.	Chtěl bych černou kávu a zmrzlinu.	*Khtyel bikh chair-now kah-voo ah zmurs-lee-noo*
* Do you want anything else?	* Přejete si ještě něco?	*pzheh-yetteh see yeshtyeh nyetsoh*
No, that's all.	Ne, to je všechno.	*neh toh yeh fshekhnoh*
Bring me	Přineste mi	*pzhinnesteh mee*
... a glass of water,	... sklenici vody	*sklennitsi voddy*
... a bottle of mineral water.	... láhev minerálky.	*läh-hef minnerählky*
Waiter (Head-waiter) the bill!	Pane vrchní,[1] platit!	*punneh verkhnee pluttit*

Names of foodstuffs and drinks are to be found on pp. 38–41.

ash tray	popelník *m.*	*poppelnyeek*
milk bar	mlékárna *f.*	*mlair-kährnah*
dinner	večeře *f.*	*veh-chezheh*
to have d.	večeřet	*veh-chezhet*

[1] When, after having finished your meal, you want to pay your bill and leave the place you must raise your fingers and say these words loudly and clearly while the waiter is passing by your table. Vrchní (literally: Chief) is the most elusive person in the whole restaurant and it is more difficult to catch his attention than to catch the waitress's eye in an English restaurant.

36

dish	**jídlo** n.	*yeedloh*
food	**jídlo, pokrm** n. m.	*pockerm*
fork	**vidlička** f.	*vidlitchkah*
knife	**nůž** m.	*noosh*
knife and fork	**příbor** m.	*psheeborr*
lunch	**oběd** m.	*obyet*
to have lunch	**obědvat**	*obyedvutt*
napkin	**ubrousek** m.	*oobrowseck*
meal	**jídlo** n.	*yeedloh*
to order	**objednat**	*obyednutt*
portion (helping)	**porce** f.	*porr-tseh*
spoon	**lžíce** f.	*lzheetseh*
supper	**večeře** f.	*veh-chezheh*
tablecloth	**ubrus** m.	*oobrooss*
tea-room (café)	**kavárna** f.	*kuvvāhr-nah*
tin (can)	**konzerva** f.	*kon-zerr-vah*
wine-list	**vinný lístek** m.	*vinnee leestek*

• A meal costs from 12 to 25 crowns (and more, in de luxe restaurants and Class A hotels). Roast pork or roast goose or duck with dumplings and sauerkraut are "the national dishes". Sirloin of beef with cream sauce and dumplings can also be recommended. Mutton is very rare, except perhaps in Slovakia where seasoned dishes and sauces, paprika salads and other vegetables make for a greater variety of restaurant cuisine. Czech beer (Pilsner and Budweisser) is exported to all parts of the world. Wine is more expensive than beer. Coffee is generally good, tea is bad.

• In the better-class wine-restaurants you will find a wide range of native and foreign wines. Wine-taverns with a lot of atmosphere have been established lately in the cellars of some medieval houses of the Old Town and the Malá Strana (Lesser Town) of Prague. "The Month in Prague" (see p. 34) will give you ample information about these places.

• Tasty fried sausages with bread and mustard can be had till the small hours at street stalls, especially in Wenceslas Square. These have always been a feature of "Prague after dark".

• Visitors with a sweet tooth will find Czech fancy pastry much to their liking.

● If you are satisfied with your food or drink, you will need the following expressions:

Some more = **ještě trochu** *yeshtyeh trokhoo*

Another: have another glass of beer **dejte si** *dayteh see* **ještě jedno pivo** *yeshtyeh yednoh peevoh*, **na můj účet** *nah mooy oochet* on me.

FOOD AND DRINK

Předkrmy	*Entrees, Hors d'Oeuvres*
Pražská šunka s křenem	Prague ham with horseradish
nebo okurkou	or cucumber (pickle)
Ruské vejce s majonézou	Egg with mayonnaise
Humrový salát	Lobster salad with
s majonézou	mayonnaise
Žampióny s vejci	Mushrooms with eggs
Omeleta s hráškem	Green pea omelette

Polévky	*Soups*
hnědá (hovězí)	Consommé (clear soup)
bílá	Thick soup
zeleninová, houbová	vegetable s., mushroom s.,
bramborová, květáková	potato s., cauliflower s.,
chřestová, hrachová,	asparagus s., pea s.,
tomatová, nudlová,	tomato s., noodle s.,
drštková	tripe s.

Ryby	*Fish*
Kapr vařený s máslem	Carp, boiled, melted butter
a brambory	and potatoes
Kapr pečený	Carp, grilled,
s opékanými brambory	roast potatoes
Kapr smažený	Carp, fried
Pstruh pečený	Trout, grilled
nebo vařený	or boiled
Fillé na rožni (smažené)	Fillet (barbecued)

Hotová jídla	*Dishes ready to be served*
Pečená husa (kachna), knedlík, zelí	Roast goose (duck), dumplings, cabbage (saur-kraut)
Kuře na rožni	Chicken, grilled
Hovězí vařené, rajská omáčka, knedlík	Boiled beef, tomato sauce, dumplings
Hovězí guláš, knedlík nebo brambor	Beef goulash, dumplings or potatoes
Svíčková na smetaně, knedlík	Sirloin of beef with cream sauce, dumplings
Roštěnka s rýží	Stewed steak, with rice
Telecí na paprice, rýže nebo makarony	Veal prepared with paprika, rice or maccaroni
Vepřová pečeně, knedlík, zelí	Roast pork, dumplings, cabbage
Čočka s vejcem	Lentils, with egg
Vařený květák s máslem	Cauliflower, boiled, melted butter

Jídla na objednávku (minutky) — *Dishes to order (ā la minute)*

Biftek s vejcem, opékané brambory	Beefsteak with egg, roast potatoes
Přírodní telecí řízek s brambory nebo rýží	Slice of veal with potatoes or rice
Smažený vepřový řízek,	Fillet of pork, fried, (Breaded cutlet)
bramborový salát	potato salad
Anglická játra	Liver à l'anglaise

Moučníky — *Sweets (Dessert)*

Čokoládový nebo kávový dort	Chocolate tart or Coffee tart (cake)
Jablkový závin	Apple roll
Rýžový nákyp	Rice pudding
Švestkové knedlíky	Little plum dumplings
Palačinky	Pancakes
Omeleta se zavařeninou	Jam omelette

Sýry — *Cheese*

Niva	Roquefort
Gouda, Eidam	Dutch cheeses
Černá nebo bílá káva	Black coffee or coffee with milk

The reputation of Czech cooking is well established abroad. In Brussels (1958) and in Montreal (1967) Czech and Slovak restaurants found favour with the international visitors to the EXPOs. (**Words which appear on the menu – pp. 38, 39 are not repeated here**).

acid	**kyselý**	*kissellee*
apple	**jablko** *n.*	*yabel-koh*
apricot	**meruňka** *f.*	*merr-oonkah*
bacon	**anglická slanina** *f.*	*anglitskäh slunninnah*
brains	**mozeček** *m.*	*mozzeh-chek*
brown	**hnědý**	*hnyeddee*
brown bread	**černý chléb** *m.*	*tchernee khlebb*
butter	**máslo** *n.*	*mähssloh*
cake	**koláč** *m.*	*kollähtch*
	dort *m.*	*dorrt*
	buchta *f.*	*bookhtah*
cherries	**třešně** *f.*	*tzheshnyeh*
chips (French fries)	**smažené brambory** *m.* (**hranůlky**)	*smuzhennair brumborry hrunnoolky*
chocolates	**bonbóny** *m.*	*bonbōhny*
cream	**smetana** *f.*	*smettunnah*
cutlet, chop	**kotleta** *f.*	*kotlettah*
egg	**vejce** *n.*	*vay-tseh*
soft boiled	**na měkko**	*nah myekkoh*
hard boiled	**na tvrdo**	*nah tverdoh*
fat	**tučný**	*toochnee*
grapes	**hrozny** *m.*	*hroz-ny*
hare	**zajíc** *m.*	*zah-yeets*
honey	**med** *m.*	*met*
hot	**horký**	*horrkee*
ice-cream	**zmrzlina** *f.*	*zmurs-lee-nah*
jam	**džem** *m.*	*dzhem*
joint	**kýta** *f.*	*keetah*
kidneys	**ledvinky** *f.*	*led-vinn-ky*
kipper	**uzenáč** *m.*	*oozennähtch*
lean	**libový**	*libbohvee*
lemon	**citrón** *m.*	*tsitrōhn*
lemonade	**limonáda** *f.*	*limmoh-nädah*

lump of sugar	**kostka cukru** *f.*	*cosst-kah tsookroo*
milk	**mléko** *n.*	*mlair-koh*
mushrooms	**houby** *f.*	*howbyh*
mustard	**hořčice** *f.*	*hozh-tchitseh*
mutton	**skopové** *n.*	*skoppovair*
nuts	**ořechy** *m.*	*ozhekhy*
onion	**cibule** *f.*	*tsibbooleh*
orange	**pomeranč** *m.*	*pomerrunch*
pepper	**pepř** *m.*	*pepzh*
pale ale (pilsener)	**světlé pivo** *n.*	*svyetlair peevoh*
peaches	**broskve** *f.*	*brosk-veh*
plums	**švestky** *f.*	*shvest-ky*
pear	**hruška** *f.*	*hrooshkah*
pheasant	**bažant** *m.*	*buzhant*
preserves (jams)	**zavařeniny**	*zuvvah-zhenniny*
rice	**rýže** *f.*	*reezheh*
roast (joint)	**pečeně** *f.*	*petchenyeh*
roll	**houska** *f.*	*howskah*
	rohlík *m.*	*roh-leek*
salmon	**losos** *m.*	*lossoss*
salt	**sůl** *f.*	*sool*
salted	**slaný**	*slunnee*
salt herring	**slaneček** *m.*	*slunnetcheck*
sauce	**omáčka** *f.*	*ommāh-chkah*
sausages (hot dogs)	**párky** *m.*	*pāhr-ky*
	špekáčky *m.*	*shpekāh-chky*
slice of bread	**krajíček**	*krah-yeechek*
	chleba *m.*	*khlebbah*
sour	**kyselý**	*kissellee*
spinach	**špenát** *m.*	*shpennāht*
spirits	**lihoviny** *f.*	*lee-hovvinny*
steak	**biftek** *m.*	
stewed fruit	**kompot** *m.*	
stout	**černý ležák** *m.*	*cherrnee lehzhāk*
strawberries	**jahody** *f.*	*ya-hoddy*
sugar	**cukr** *m.*	*tsookerr*
sweet	**sladký**	*slut-kee*
vinegar	**ocet** *m.*	*otset*
whipped cream	**šlehačka** *f.*	*shleh-hutchkah*
tongue	**jazyk** *m.*	*yah-zyk*
turkey	**krůta** *f.*	*krootah*
to drink	**pít**	*peet*

KAVÁRNA	Café
VINÁRNA	Wine cellar
MLÉČNÝ BAR	Milk bar
CHLÉB A PEČIVO	Bread and Pastry
AUTOMAT (BUFET)	Snack-bar
MASO A UZENINY	Meat and Charcuterie (salamis)
STUDENÁ JÍDLA	Cold Dishes
JÍDELNA	Eating-place
NEALKOHOLICKÉ NÁPOJE	Soft Drinks
OVOCE A ZELENINA	Fruit and Vegetables
DRŮBEŽ RYBY	Poultry Fish
ZVĚŘINA	Venison
STUDENÉ A TEPLÉ NÁPOJE	Cold and Warm Drinks
CUKRÁRNA	Confectionery (candy store
CUKROVINKY	Sweets
SAMOOBSLUHA	Supermarket
POTRAVINY	Grocery, Provisions
LAHŮDKY	Delicacies (Delicatessen)
NÁPOJE	Beverages
POLOTOVARY	Semi-prepared Foodstuffs (ready for cooking)

AT THE HAIRDRESSER'S, TAKING A BATH, AT THE DRY-CLEANER'S

| I want my hair washed and set. | **Potřebuji umýt vlasy a vodovou ondulaci.** | *potzhebbooyi oomeet vlussy ah voddohvow ondoolutsi* |

| * Haircut or shave, Sir? A light trim at the back and sides. | * **Stříhat nebo holit, prosím? Jen přistřihnout vzadu a po stranách.** | *stzheehut nebboh hollit prosseem yen pzhi-stzhih-nowt vzuddoo ah postrunnäkh* |

| Not too short in front. | **Ne moc zkrátka vpředu.** | *neh mots skräht-kah fpzheddoo* |

| I should like to have a wash (a bath). I have had an accident. | **Chtěl bych se umýt (se vykoupat). Měl jsem úraz.** | *khtyel bikh seh oomeet seh vikkowputt mnyel sem ooruss* |

May I have hot water, soap and a towel?	**Můžu dostat horkou vodu, mýdlo a ručník?**	*moozhoo dostut horrkow voddoo meedloh ah rootch-neek*
* Certainly, sir.	* **Jistě, pane.**	*yistyeh punneh*
* Here you are.	* **Prosím.**	*prosseem*
Thank you.	**Děkuji vám.**	*dyekoo-yi vāhm*
It's very kind of you.	**Jste velmi laskav (laskavá).**[1]	*steh velmee luskuf (luskuvvāh)*
I wish to have:	**Přeju si:**	*pzeh-yoo see*
my shirt washed	**vyprat košili**	*vipprut koshilly*
my trousers pressed	**vyžehlit kalhoty**	*vizheh-lit kulhotty*
my shoes cleaned.	**vyčistit boty.**	*vitchistit botty*
Please wash carefully!	**Perte prosím opatrně!**	*perrteh prosseem opah-ternyeh*
Would you kindly sew on this button?	**Můžete mi laskavě přišít knoflík?**	*moozhetteh mee luskuvvyeh pzhisheet knofleek*
remove this stain?	**vyčistit skvrnu?**	*vitchistit skvernoo*
bandage dressing	**obvaz** *m.*	*obvuss*
collar	**límec** *m.*	*leemets*
comb	**hřeben** *m.*	*zhebben*
to comb	**učesat**	*oochessut*
eau de Cologne	**kolínská voda** *f.*	*colleenskah voddah*
face	**obličej** *m.*	*oblitchay*
face powder	**pudr** *m.*	*pooderr*
a hairdo	**učesání** *n.*	*oochessāhnee*
iron	**žehlička** *f.*	*zheh-litchkah*
insoles	**vložky do bot** *f.*	*vloshky dobbot*
linen	**prádlo** *n.*	*prāh-dloh*
lipstick	**rtěnka**	*rr-tyenkah*
needle	**jehla** *f.*	*yeh-hlah*
perfume	**voňavka** *f.*	*vonyafkah*
a perm	**trvalá**	*tervullāh*

---

[1] **Laskav** for a man; **laskavá** for a woman.

44

patent fastener (snap)	**patentka** *f.*	*puttentkah*
pocket	**kapsa** *f.*	*kup-sah*
pocket-mirror	**kapesní zrcátko** *n.*	*kupessnee zertsāht-koh*
razor-blades	**žiletky** *f.*	*zhilletky*
safety pin	**spínací špendlík** *m.*	*speenutsee shpendleek*
paper	**papír**	*puppeer*
safety razor	**holicí strojek** *m.*	*hollitsee stroyek*
scissors	**nůžky**	*nooshky*
shampoo	**šampón** *m.*	*shumpōhn*
shoebrush	**kartáč na boty**	*kahr-tāhtch nahbotty*
shoe-lace	**tkaničky do bot** *f.*	*kunnyitchky dobbot*
straight razor	**břitva** *f.*	*bzhitvah*
sunglasses	**brýle proti slunci**	*breeleh protti sloontsi*
thread	**nit** *f.*	*nyit*
toilet soap	**toaletní mýdlo** *n.*	*toah-letnee meedloh*
toothbrush	**kartáček na zuby** *m.*	*karr-tāh-chek nahzooby*
toothpaste	**pasta na zuby** *f.*	*pahstah nahzooby*

PARNÍ A VANOVÉ LÁZNĚ	Public Baths
KADEŘNICTVÍ	Hairdresser
PRANÍ A ŽEHLENÍ PRÁDLA	Laundry and Ironing
RYCHLOČISTÍRNA	Dry Cleaners
HOLIČSTVÍ	Barber
DROGERIE	Chemist (Drugstore)
OPRAVA OBUVI (na počkání)	Shoe Repairs (while you wait)
ZAKÁZKOVÉ KREJČOVSTVÍ	(Custom Tayloring)

SHOPPING

See also: The First Steps, At a Restaurant.

Where can I get	**Kde dostanu**	*gdeh dostunnoo*
records	**desky**	*desky*
of Czech music,	**české hudby,**	*chesskair hoodbee*
Slovak dolls,	**slovenské**	*slovvenskair*
	panenky,	*punnenky*
old coins?	**staré mince?**	*stah-rair mintseh*
Is there any shop	**Je nějaký obchod**	*yeh nye-yuckee*
selling...	**s...**	*op-khot*

How much is	**Kolik stojí**	*kollick stoyee*
this tea-set?	**ten čajový**	*ten tchah-yovvee*
	servis?	*serrviss*
It's too expensive.	**To je moc**	*toh yeh mots*
	drahé.	*drah-hēh*
Show me	**Ukažte mi**	*ookushteh mee*
something else	**něco jiného**	*nyetsoh yeenair-hoh*

(something better).	(něco lepšího).	*nyetsoh lepshee-hoh*
Wrap it up	Zabalte to	*zubbulteh toh*
carefully.	pečlivě.	*pech-livvyeh*
It's a present.	Je to dárek.	*yeh toh dāh-rek*
Send it	Pošlete to	*poshletteh toh*
to my address.	na mou adresu.	*nah mow udressoo*
What time	V kolik hodin	*fkollick hoddin*
do shops close?	se zavírají	*seh zuvveerah-yee*
	obchody?	*op-khody*
* At six p. m.	* V šest hodin	*fshest hoddin*
	večer.	*vetcherr*
When do they	Kdy se otvírají?	*gdy seh otveerah-yee*
open?		
* At eight a. m.	* V osm hodin	*f ossoom hoddin*
	ráno.	*rāh-noh*
Can I have this	Můžete mi ten	*moozhetteh mee ten*
film developed?	film vyvolat?	*film vivvollut*
When will it be	Kdy to bude	*gdy toh boodeh*
ready?	hotovo?	*hottovvoh*
Make	Udělejte	*oodyellayteh*
three prints	tři kopie	*tzhee koppee-yeh*
of each snapshot.	od každého	*ot kuzh-dair-hoh*
	snímku.	*snyeemkoo*

Weights and measures:

a pound	půl kila (circa)	*pool killah*
two pounds	kilo *n.* (circa)	*killoh*
100 grams	deset deka	*desset dekkah*
50 grams	pět deka	*pyet dekkah*
a dozen	tucet *m.*	*tootset*
a small parcel	balíček *m.*	*bulleecheck*
a pint	půl litru (circa)	*pool littroo*
two pints	litr *m.* (circa)	*litrr*
half a pint	čtvrt litru (circa)	*shtverrt littroo*
two decilitres	dvě deci	*dvyeh detsi*
a piece	kus *m.*	*kooss*
a bit	kousek *m.*	*kowsseck*
a pair	pár *m.*	*pahrr*
bathing costume	plavky	*plufky*
(suit)		
belt, girdle	pás *m.*	*pāhss*

suspender	podvazkový	podvuskovee
(stocking) belt	pás m.	pāhs
blouse	bluza f.	bloozah
brassière	podprsenka f.	pot-persenkah
to buy	(na)koupit	(nah)kowpit
candle	svíčka f.	sveetchkah
cigar	doutník m.	dowtnyeek
cloth, fabrics	látky f.	lāhtky
clothes	šaty f.	shutty
coat	plášť m.	plāhsht
colour film	barevný film m.	bahr-evnee film
cotton	bavlna f.	bah-velnah
diary	zápisník m.	zah-pissnyeek
dress, suit	šaty, oblek m.	shutty, obleck
dressing gown	župan m.	zhoopun
envelope	obálka f.	obāhlkah
filter-tipped	cigarety	tsigaretty
cigarettes	s filtrem f.	sfiltr-ehm
fountain pen	plnicí péro n.	pelnyi-tsee pairoh
frock	dámské šaty f.	dāhmskeh shutty
gloves	rukavice f.	rookuvvitseh
handbag	kabelka f.	kubbelkah
handkerchief	kapesník m.	kuppesnyeek
hat	klobouk m.	kloobowk
jacket	sako n.	suckoh
lighter	zapalovač m.	zuppullohvutch
matches	zápalky f.	zāhpulky
notepaper	dopisní papír m.	doppissnyee
(stationary)		puppeerr
packing paper	balící papír m.	bullitsee puppeerr
panties	kalhotky f.	kulhotky
pencil	tužka f.	tooshkah
playing cards	hrací karty f.	hrutsee karrty
price	cena f.	tsennah
purse	peněženka f.	pennyeh-zhenkah
receipt	stvrzenka f.	stver-zenkah
roll-film	svitkový film m.	svitkovee film
sale	výprodej m.	veeprodday
sanitary towel (pad)	dámská	dāhmskāh
	vložka f.	vloshkah
scarf	šála f.	shāhlah
to sell	prodávat	proddāhvut

shirt	**košile** *f.*	*koshilleh*
shoes	**boty**	*botty*
shop assistant	**prodavač** *m.*	*prodduvvutch*
skirt	**sukně** *f.*	*sooknyeh*
slacks	**kalhoty** *f.*	*kulhotty*
slip	**kombiné** *n.*	*kombinnair*
slippers	**trepky**	*trepky*
socks	**ponožky**	*ponnoshky*
stockings	**punčochy**	*poon-chokhy*
tie	**vázanka**	*vähzunkah*
	kravata *f.*	*kruvattah*
thread (cord)	**provázek** *m.*	*proh-vähzeck*
trousers	**kalhoty**	*kulhotty*
umbrella	**deštník** *m.*	*deshtnyeek*
underwear	**spodní prádlo** *n.*	*spodnyee prähdloh*
woman's vest (undershirt)	**dámská košile** *f.*	*dähmskah koshilleh*
wallet	**náprsní**	*näh-pers-nyee*
	taška *f.*	*tushkah*
watch	**hodinky**	*hoddinky*
wool	**vlna** *f.*	*velnah*
woollen	**vlněný**	*velnyennee*

Some colours:

black	**černý**	*chairnee*
white	**bílý**	*beelee*
green	**zelený**	*zellennee*
blue	**modrý**	*modree*
dark	**tmavý**	*tmuvvee*
red	**červený**	*chairvennee*
gray	**šedý**	*sheddee*
yellow	**žlutý**	*zhlootee*
pink	**růžový**	*roozhovvee*
light	**světlý**	*svyetlee*

PÁNSKÉ ODĚVY A PRÁDLO	Men's Wear
PÁNSKÁ OBUV	Men's Footwear
SKLO A PORCELÁN	Glass and China
STAROŽITNOSTI	Antiques
POTŘEBY PRO DOMÁCNOST	Household Goods

TABÁK	Tobacconist
DOPLŇKY	Accessories
KOŽENÉ ZBOŽÍ	Leather Goods
ANTIKVARIÁT	Second-hand Books
KNIHY	
A HUDEBNINY	Books and Music
PARTIOVÉ ZBOŽÍ	Bargains
NOVINY A ČASOPISY	Newspapers
(Poštovní a novinová služba,	and Periodicals
PNS)	
PÁNSKÉ A DÁMSKÉ	
PRÁDLO	Men's and Women's
	Underwear
GALANTERIE	Haberdashery (Notions)
PAPÍRNICTVÍ	Stationery
KVĚTINY	Flowers
HUDEBNÍ NÁSTROJE	Musical Instruments
HODINY A KLENOTY	Watches and Jewels

OFFICES (Customs, Post-office, Bank)

English	Czech	Pronunciation
* Have you anything to declare?	* **Máte něco k proclení?**	*māhteh nyetsoh k prots-lennyee*
* Open this suitcase.	* **Otevřte ten kufřík.**	*otevzhteh ten koofzheek*
I want to send a telegram.	**Chci poslat telegram.**	*kh-tsee poslut tellegrum*

English	Czech	Pronunciation
Reply pre-paid.	**S placenou odpovědí.**	*splutsennow otpovyedyee*
I need stamps for two ordinary letters.	**Potřebuji známky na dva obyčejné dopisy.**	*potzebbooyi znāhmky nah dvah obitchay-nair dopissy*
* Foreign or inland?	* **Do ciziny nebo do Československa?**	*doh tsizinny nebboh doh chesskoh-slovenskah*
How much is it alltogether?	**Kolik to dělá dohromady?**	*kollick toh dyelāh doh-hromuddy*

English	Czech	Pronunciation
I should like to have a trunkcall (long distance call) put through to... as a personal call	Chtěl bych telefonovat meziměstsky do... na výzvu.	khtyel bikh tellefoh-nohvut mezzee-myestky doh... nah veezvoo
* There is no reply.	* Nikdo se nehlásí.	nigdoh seh neh-hlāhssee
* Number engaged.	* Je obsazeno.	yeh opsuzzennoh
* Will you wait?	* Počkáte si?	potch-kāhteh see
Put me through to Mr. Black.	Spojte mě s panem Černým.	spoyteh mnyeh spunnem Cherneem
Where can I change some money?	Kde si můžu vyměnit peníze?	gdeh see moozhoo vimmyenit pennyeezeh
I have lost my passport.	Ztratil jsem cestovní pas.	struttil sem tsestovnyee puss
* You must report it to the police.	* Musíte to ohlásit na policii.	moosseeteh toh oh-hlāhssit nah pollittsi-yee
Are you on the phone?	Máte telefon?	māhteh tellefõhn
You are wanted on the phone!	Máte tady telefon!	māhteh tuddy tellefonn
Radio	rozhlas m.	roz-hluss
broadcasting	vysílání n.	visseelāhnyee
by airmail	letecky	lettetsky
foreign	cizí	tsizzee
currency	valuty f.	vullooty
interpreter	tlumočník m.	tloomotchnyeek
letter-box (mail box)	poštovní schránka f.	poshtovnyee skhrāhnkah
letter of credit	akreditiv m.	uckredditeef
local call	místní hovor m.	meestnyee hovvorr
office	úřad m. kancelář f.	oozhut kuntselāhzh
picture post-card	pohlednice f.	poh-hlednyitseh
postcard	dopisnice f.	doppisnitseh
postage	poštovné	poshtovnair
postal order	poštovní poukázka f.	poshtovnyee poh-ookāhsskah

passport control	**pasová**	*pussováh*	
	kontrola *f.*	*kontrollah*	
press	**tisk** *m.*	*tyisk*	
printed matter	**tiskovina** *f.*	*tiskovvinnah*	
rate of exchange	**kurs deviz** *m.*	*koors devvees*	
sender	**odesílatel** *m.*	*oddesseeluttel*	
signature	**podpis** *m.*	*potpiss*	
small change	**drobné** *n.*	*drobnair*	
telephone box	**telefonní budka** *f.*	*tellephonnee bootkah*	
tel. directory	**telefonní**	*tellephonnee*	
	seznam *m.*	*seznum*	
traveller's cheque (check)	**cestovní šek** *m.*	*tsestovnyee shek*	
wireless	**rádio** *n.*	*rahdeeoh*	

DOPORUČENĚ	Registered
SMĚNÁRNA	Money Exchange
VKLADY A VÝPLATY	Deposits and Withdrawals
SPOŘITELNA	Savings-bank
STÁTNÍ BANKA	State Bank
VEŘEJNÁ BEZPEČNOST (VB)	Police
ZDRAVOTNICTVÍ	Public Health
MINISTERSTVO ZAHRANIČNÍCH VĚCÍ	Ministry of Foreign Affairs
TELEFON K POUŽITÍ	You may 'phone here
VÝZKUMNÝ ÚSTAV	Research Institute
KONZULÁT	Consulate
VELVYSLANECTVÍ	Embassy

● For public phone boxes you need a fifty heller coin. Most cafés and restaurants have tin-tag operated phones; the token can usually be obtained from the cloakroom attendant.

When does ... begin?	**Kdy začíná...?**	*gdy zutcheenāh...*
When does ... end?	**Kdy končí...?**	*gdy kontchee*
I want two tickets.	**Potřebuji dvě místa.**	*pot-zhebbooyi dvyeh meestah*
Orchestra stalls, for ...	**Křesla na...**	*kzheslah nah...*
* Sold out.	*** Je vyprodáno.**	*yeh vipproddāhnoh*
Is this Italian film in the original version?	**Je ten italský film v původní verzi?**	*yeh ten itulskee film fpoovodnee verrzee*

| * No, it has been dubbed in Czech. | *** Ne, je namluven česky.** | *neh yeh numlooven chessky* |
| Where can I listen to church music? | **Kde můžu poslouchat kostelní hudbu?** | *gdeh moozhoo poslowkhut kostelnyee hoodboo* |

* At St. James's.	* U svatého Jakuba.	*oo svuttair-hoh yuckoobah*
Is there any foreign language bookshop in Prague?	Je v Praze cizojazyčné knihkupectví?	*yeh fprah-zeh tsizzoh-yah-zitchnair knih-koopetstvee*
* Yes, near the Powder Tower.	* Ano, u Prašné brány.	*unnoh oo prushnair bräh-ny*
I'd like to see an exhibition of modern Czech painting.	Přeju si vidět výstavu moderního českého malířství.	*pzheh-yoo see viddyet veestuvvoo moderrneehoh chesskair-hoh mulleezh-stvee*
Have you got records of folk music?	Máte desky lidové hudby?	*mähteh desky liddovvair hoodby*
* Yes, we have new recordings.	* Ano, máme nové nahrávky.	*unnoh mähmeh novvair nah-hrähfky*
Where can I get an English Guide to the National Gallery?	Kde dostanu anglického průvodce po Národní galerii?	*gdeh dostunnoo unglitskair-hoh proovotseh poh näh-rod-nyee gullerri-yee*
Can you get me four tickets for the concert?	Můžete mi obstarat čtyři lístky na koncert?	*moozhetteh mee opstah-rut shtirshee leestky nah kontsert*
act	jednání n.	*yednähnee*
actor	herec m.	*herrets*
actress	herečka f.	*herretchkah*
ballet	balet m.	*bahlet*
booking-office	prodej vstupenek m.	*prodday fstoopennek*
advance booking	předprodej m.	*pzhedprodday*
box	lóže f.	*lōh-zheh*
cash-desk (box office)	pokladna f.	*pockludnah*
cinema	kino n. biograf m.	*kinnoh beeograph*
comedy	veselohra f.	*vesselo-hrah*

55

dress-circle	první balkón *m.*	*perv-nnyee bullköhn*
emergency exit	nouzový východ *m.*	*nowzovvee veekhot*
feature film	hlavní film *m.*	*hluvnyee film*
first night	premiéra *f.*	*prenni-airah*
interval (intermission)	přestávka *f.*	*pzhestähfkah*
musical	opereta *f.* muzikál *m.*	*operrettah moozikkähl*
newsreel	obrazový týdeník *m.*	*obruzzovvee teedennyeek*
opera-glasses	kukátko *n.*	*kookähtkoh*
open-air theatre	divadlo *n.* v přírodě	*deevudloh fpzhee-roddyeh*
performance	představení *n.*	*pzhet-stuvvenyee*
pit (orchestra)	přízemí *n.*	*pzheezemmee*
play	hra *f.*	*hrah*
to play	hrát	*hräht*
	já hraju	*hrah-yoo*
	vy hrajete	*hrah-yetteh*
poster	plakát *m.*	*pluckäht*
song	píseň *f.*	*peesenye*

- Czech films have been awarded many prizes at international festivals. The Magic Lantern, a combination of stage and film art, was an outstanding success at the Montreal EXPO 67.

- The collections of Czech Gothic art at the National Gallery (especially the beautiful Bohemian Madonnas) are well worth seeing.

- "The Month in Prague" (p. 34) gives you full particulars about museums, concert-halls, theatres and art galleries. In L. Motka's guidebook (p. 6) you will find (pp. 11–17) a description of Czech and Slovak folklore.

- You may not smoke in theatres or cinemas. Late comers are not admitted to their seats and have to wait for an interval.

Is the Vltava deep?	**Je Vltava hluboká?**	*yeh veltah-vah hloobockāh*
* It is not, but the water is cold.	* **Není, ale voda je studená.**	*nennyee ulleh voddah yeh stoodennāh*
* I recommend you the new swimming-pool at Podolí.	* **Doporučuji vám novou plovárnu v Podolí.**	*dopporoo-tchooyi vāhm novvow plovvāhrnoo f poddollee*

| When does the final take place? | **Kdy se hraje finále?** | *gdy seh hrah-yeh finnāhleh* |
| Who is playing whom? | **Kdo hraje s kým?** | *gdoh hrah-yeh skeem* |

I should like	Chtěl bych	kh-tyel bikh
to make a trip	udělat výlet	oodyelut veelet
by steamboat.	parníkem.	parr-neekem
Is it possible to	Je možné vidět	yeh mozhnair
see any folk-dances	v Praze nějaké	viddyet fprah-zeh
in Prague	lidové tance	nye-yuckair
		liddovair tuntseh
(national	(národní	(nährodnyee
costumes)	kroje)	kroyeh)
* Yes, certainly.	* Ano, jistě.	unnoh yistyeh
When is open	Kdy je otevřen	gdy yeh otev-zhen
the ... palace?	... palác?	... pah-lähts
the ... library?	Kdy je otevřena	
	... knihovna?	... kneehovvnah
the ... museum?	Kdy je otevřeno	
	... museum?	... moo-zeh-oom
* On Mondays	* V pondělí	fpondyellee
museums are	jsou muzea	sow moo-zeh-hah
closed.	zavřena.	zuv-zhennah

• During the summer months, folk dances in national costumes are performed by the Czechoslovak State Folk Song and Dance Ensemble on Žofín, a little Vltava islet (five minutes' walk from the National Theatre). You should inquire about the dates of performances.

ball	míč m.	meech
to bathe	koupat se	kowput seh
to borrow	vypůjčit si	vippooy-chit see
chess	šachy	shah-khy
dance	tanec m.	tunnets
to dance	tančit	tunchit
deck chair	lehátko n.	leh-hähtkoh
figure skating	krasobruslení n.	krussoh-brooslennyee
game	hra f.	hrah
golf links	golfové hřiště n.	golfovvair h-zheeshtyeh
gymnastics	tělocvik m.	tyelloh-tsvik
a jump	skok m.	skock

match	zápas m.	zăh-puss
nightclub	noční bar	notchnee bar
playground	hřiště n.	h-zheestyeh
puppet-show	loutkové	lowtkovvair
	divadlo n.	deevudloh
rowing	veslování n.	vesslovvăhnee
skating	bruslení	broosslennee
skating-ring	kluziště n.	kloozishtyeh
to shoot	střílet	stzhee-let
ski	lyže	leezheh
skiing	lyžování n.	leezhovvăhnyee
stadium	stadión m.	studdy-ōhn
team	mužstvo n.	moosh-stvoh
trip	výlet m.	veelet
referee	soudce m.	sowtseh
wind	vítr m.	veetr
winter sports	zimní sporty	zimnyee sporrty
world	svět m.	svyet

| JARO | LÉTO | PODZIM | ZIMA |
| Spring | Summer | Autumn | Winter |

| ZEMĚ | SLUNCE | MĚSÍC | HVĚZDA |
| Earth | Sun | Moon | Star |

| SEVER | JIH | ZÁPAD | VÝCHOD |
| North | South | West | East |

Some "meteorological" terms:

climate	podnebí n.	podnebbee
cloud	mrak m.	mruk
fire	oheň m.	oh-henye
fog	mlha f.	melhah
flame	plamen m.	plummen
light	světlo n.	svyetloh
mud	bláto n.	blăhtoh
rain	déšt m.	dair-sht
it rains	prší	per-shee
shadow	stín m.	styeen
sky	nebe n.	nebbeh
	obloha f.	obloh-hah

snow	**sníh** *m.*	*snyeekh*
it is snowing	**sněží**	*snyezhee*
weather	**počasí** *n.*	*potchussee*
It is warm	**je teplo**	*yeh teploh*
It is cold	**je zima**	*yeh zimmah*
I am warm	**je mi teplo**	*yeh me teploh*
I am cold	**je mi zima**	*yeh me zimmah*
It's a fine day	**je hezky**	*yeh hessky*
A nasty day	**je ošklivo**	*yeh oshklivvoh*

AT A DOCTOR'S

Call in a doctor!	**Zavolejte lékaře!**	*zuvvollayteh laikrahzheh*
At once!	**Ihned!**	*ih-net*
* What's the trouble?	* **Co je vám?**	*tsoh yet vāhm*
	* **Co vás bolí?**	*tsoh vāhss bollee*
It hurts me here.	**Bolí mě tady.**	*bollee mnyeh tuddy*

* You must have a rest, keep to your bed.	* **Musíte si odpočinout, zůstat v posteli.**	*moosseeteh see otpotchinnowt zoostut fpostelly*
How often shall I take this medicine?	**Jak často mám brát ten lék?**	*yuck chusstoh māhm brāht ten lairk*
* Three times a day after meals before meals	* **Třikrát denně po jídle před jídlem**	*tzhikrāht dennyeh poyeedleh pzhed yeedlem*

When shall I call again?	Kdy mám zase přijít?	gdy máhm zusseh pzhi-yeet
* In three days.	* Za tři dny.	zah tzhee dny
I have a toothache	Bolí mě zub.	bollee mnyeh zoop
Which are the dentist's consultation hours?	Kdy ordinuje zubní lékař?	gdy ordinnooyeh zoobnyee lairkazh
* From 8 to 10, every day except Sundays.	* Od osmi do deseti každý den kromě neděle.	otosmee doh desseti kuzhdee den kromyeh neddyelleh
Can this tooth be filled?	Může se ten zub plombovat?	moozheh seh ten zoop plombovvut
* I must pull it out.	* Musím ho vytáhnout.	moosseem hoh vittáh-nowt
Give me something against headache	Dejte mi něco proti bolení hlavy	dayteh mee nyetsoh protti bollennyee hlav-vy
against coughing.	proti kašli.	protti kushly
abscess	vřed m.	vzhet
bleeding	krvácení n.	kerváh-tsennyee
blood	krev f.	kref
bone	kost f.	
a cold	nachlazení n.	nukh-luzzennyee
compress	obklad m.	opklutt
concussion of the brain	otřes mozku	otzhess mosskoo
constipation	zácpa f.	záhts-pah
cotton wool	vata f.	vuttah
cramp	křeč f.	kzhetch
diarrhoea	průjem m.	proo-yem
diet	dieta f.	dee-yettah
dizziness	závrať f.	záh-vrut
dressing	obvaz m.	obvuss
ear	ucho n.	oo-khoh
eye	oko n.	ockoh
faint	omdlení n.	omdlennyee
finger	prst m.	perst
fever	horečka f.	horretchkah
flu	chřipka f.	kh-zhipkah
hospital	nemocnice f.	nehmots-nitseh
heart	srdce n.	sertseh

hand	**ruka** *f.*	*rookah*
health	**zdraví** *n.*	*zdruvvee*
infirmary	**ošetřovna** *f.*	*oshet-zhovnah*
inflammation	**zánět** *m.*	*zāh-nyet*
injury	**úraz** *m.*	*ooruss*
	poranění *n.*	*porrunyennyee*
laxative	**projimadlo** *n.*	*proyeemudloh*
leg	**noha** *f.*	*noh-hah*
lungs	**plíce**	*pleetseh*
medecine	**lék** *m.*	*lairk*
nose	**nos** *m.*	*noss*
neck	**krk** *m.*	*kerrk*
nurse	**sestra** *f.*	*sestrah*
ointment	**mast** *f.*	*must*
optician	**optika** *f.*	*optickah*
pain, ache	**bolest** *f.*	*bollest*
prescription	**recept** *m.*	*reh-tsept*
poisoning	**otrava** *m.*	*otruvvah*
shoulder	**rameno** *n.*	*rummennoh*
to sleep	**spát**	*spāht*
a sore throat	**bolení v krku** *n.*	*fkerkoo*
stomach	**žaludek** *m.*	*zhulloodek*
surgeon	**chirurg** *m.*	*khee-roork*
surgery	**ordinace** *f.*	*orrdinnutseh*
temperature	**zvýšená**	*zveeshennāh*
	teplota	*teplottah*
healthy	**zdravý**	*zdruvvee*
ill	**nemocný**	*nehmotsnee*
thermometer	**teploměr** *m.*	*teploh-mnyerr*
throat	**hrdlo** *n.*	*herr-dloh*
urine	**moč** *f.*	*motch*
vomiting	**zvracení** *n.*	*zvrutsennyee*

AMBULANCE	Out-patients' Dept.
PRVNÍ POMOC	First Aid
LÉKÁRNA	Pharmacy
DĚTSKÝ LÉKAŘ	Children's Specialist (Pediatrician)

The following remarks are intended for the **hearer** and presented from the **hearer's** point of view. Those who wish to go further may acquire either W. R. and Z. Lee's **Teach Yourself Czech** (The English Universities Press, London) or Miloš Sova's **A Practical Czech Course for English-speaking Students,** Prague (2nd ed. 1962, with Key and Vocabulary).

Grammatical gender

Czech nouns are masculine, feminine or neuter. Their gender must be looked up in a dictionary.

Adjectives agree in gender with their nouns:

day	dobr-**ý** den	– masc. adj. with masc. noun
good coffee	dobr-**á** káva	– femin. adj. with femin. noun
beer	dobr-**é** pivo	– neuter adj. with neuter noun

Some adjectives have only **one** form (ending in **-í**) for all three genders:
večerní oblek (m.), evening dress; večerní Praha (f.); večerní kino (n.)

The, this, that = **ten** (masc.) ten pán, that gentleman
                ta (femin.) ta paní, that lady
                to (neuter) to město, that town

There is no article in Czech. **Město** means town, the town, a town, depending on the general sense implied by the context. **Ten, ta, to** often stand for the English definite article. The indefinite article may be rendered by **nějaký** (*nye-yuckee* = = a, some, a kind of), and sometimes also by **jeden** (= one): je tady nějaký (or: jeden) pán, there is a man here, nějaká (or: jedna) slečna, a young lady.

Possessive pronouns (adjectives)

Můj (m.), **má** or **moje** (f.), **mé** or **moje** (n.) – my, mine.
Pl. **moji** f. n. **moje**
Náš (m.), **naše** (f.), **naše** (n.) – our, ours. Pl. **naši** F. n.: **naše**
Váš (m.), **vaše** (f.), **vaše** (n.) – your, yours. Pl. **vaši** F., n.:
vaše
Jeho his; **její** *yeh-yee* her, hers. Pl. **jejich** their(s).

Interrogative pronouns

Kdo? Who? – **Koho?** Whom? – **Komu?** To whom? –
O kom? About whom? **S kým?** With whom?
Co? What? – **O čem?** About what? – **S čím?** With what?
Který? Which one? – **Jaký?** What kind of…? What like…?

Indefinite pronouns	**"Negative" pronouns**
ně- *nye-*: někdo somebody someone	**ni-** ni-kdo no-one, nobody
ně-co something	ni-c *nits* nothing
ně-jaký some, a kind of	**žádný** no
ně-který some (of a number of persons or things)	

Two negatives: **Nevím o tom nic,** I don't know anything
about it. – Hledáte někoho? Are you looking for someone? –
Nehledám **ni**koho. I am not looking for anyone.

Verbs

If you listen to questions people are asking you or to their
requests you will often hear the syllable – **te** *teh* at the end
of the verbs:

a) má**te** čas? have you any time to spare? Ví**te** to? Do you
know it?

b) přines-**te** mi… bring me… Dovol-**te!** Allow me…
Promiň-**te!**

a) In questions and statements (the Indicative, "fact-
mood"), this -**te** *teh* is preceded by a vowel (**á, e, í**):
-á**te** *āhteh*: hled-á**te** mě? Are you looking for me?
-e**te** *etteh*: jd-e**te** do hotelu? Are you going to the hotel?

-íte *eeteh*: mluv-íte česky? Do you speak Czech?

b) In requests (the Imperative mood), **-te** *teh* is preceded by a **consonant:**[1] dovol-te! promiň-te! (in Questions, there would be a vowel: dovol-íte? promin-ete? Will you allow me...? Will you excuse me?). Nemluv-te tak rychle! Don't speak so quickly! Vy mluv-íte moc rychle, you are speaking too fast.

The Present tense (See p. 25, the conjugation of "**mám**").[2]

1st group (-á)	2nd group (-í)	3rd group (-e)
(já) hled-**ám**	(já) mluv-**ím**	(já) jd-**u**
I am looking for	I am speaking	I am going
(vy) hled-**áte**	(vy) mluv-**íte**	(vy) jd-**ete**
you are looking for	you are speaking	you are going

Ex. Koho vol**áte**? Whom are **you** calling? – Vol**ám** pana Nováka. **I** am calling Mr. Novák. – Kouř-**íte**? Do **you** smoke? – Děkuj-**u** (or: děkuj-**i**, a soft ending), nekouř**ím**. No, thank you, I do not smoke. – Jed**ete** do Brna? Are **you** going (travelling) to Brno? – Ne, jedu do Bratislavy. No, I'm going to Bratislava.

Personal pronouns (já, vy, etc.) may be left out. They are only used when special stress is needed, i. e. in opposition and contrast: **já** vás znám, **I** know you; ale **vy**, but **you** mě neznáte, do not know me.

The Infinitive (The basic form you find in the Dictionary).

It ends in **-t** (or **-ti**, which is the older literary form).
1st group (the **-á** group, see above): **-at** (*hled-at*)
2nd group (the **-í** group): **-it**: *mluv-it* to speak
　　　　　　　　or **-et**: *rozum-ět* to understand
3rd group (the **-e** group) has various infinitive forms which cannot be satisfactorily identified from the Present.[3]

---

[1] With some verbs, you will find **-ěte**: jděte domů! *dyetteh domoo* go home! jdete *detteh* domů? are you going home?

[2] All persons are given there. For the traveller's needs, the 1st person singular (já) and the 2nd person plural (vy) will be sufficient on most ocasions.

[3] E. G. nés-**t** to carry (já nes-**u**, vy nes-**ete**); děk-**ovat** to thank (já děkuj-**i** or děkuj-**u**, vy děkuj-**ete**), etc.

The Infinitive form must be known for three main reasons:

a) you have to use it after the so-called modal verbs (I can, I must, I may, I want – můž-u, mus-ím, sm-ím, chc-i, můž-ete mi to ukázat? Can you show it to me?

b) it serves to form the FUTURE TENSE of the so-called imperfective verbs,[1] in combination with the auxiliary verb **"budu"**: Co bud**e**te dělat dnes večer? What will **you** be doing tonight? – Bud**u** psát dopisy **I** shall write (or: be writing) letters. **Budu** by itself (without any Infinitive) means **I shall be**. Ex. **Budete** doma? Will **you** be at home? – Ano, bud**u**. Ne, nebud**u**.

c) it gives you the clue to the PAST TENSE of verbs: You change the final **-t** of the Infinitive to **-l** (mluvi-t – mluvil) and add the auxiliary verb **"jsem"** (for the 1st person) and **"jste"** (for the 2nd person plural):

mluvil **jsem** (a woman says: mluvi-la jsem) I spoke. Ex. Mluvil **jste** s panem vedoucím? Did **you** speak to the manager?

Some more or less **irregular forms:**

byl **jsem** I was (I have been, I had been). Byl **jste** včera doma? Were **you** at home yesterday? – Ano, byl. Ne nebyl (jsem). Měl **jsem** I had. – Neměl jsem čas. I had no time.

šel **jsem** I went (a woman says: šla jsem). Kam **jste** šel? Where did **you** go? – Šel **jsem** do kina. I went to the cinema.

Compounds: ode-šel **jsem,** I went away. **On** odešel **he** went away.

při-šel **jsem,** I came. – Kdy **jste** přišel? When did you come?

jel **jsem** I went (somewhere by a vehicle, see p. 30)

Compounds: od-jel **jsem** I left (do Brna for Brno)

při-jel **jsem** I arrived.

---

[1] Imperfective verbs express incomplete, continuous or repeated actions; perfective verbs express finished or complete actions with a view to their result. This is of course only a rough-and-ready distinction and much practice is needed to master this difficult part of Czech (and generally Slavonic) grammar. The perfective verbs cannot be combined with "budu"; they have in themselves a futural meaning: koupím I shall buy; pojedu I shall go (travel); půjdu spát I shall go to bed; přijdete? will you come?

Jedl jsem I ate. Ex. Co **jste** jedl? what did **you** eat?
mohl jsem I could. – Nemohl **jsem** přijít. **I** could not come. –
* Proč **jste** nemohl? Why couldn't **you?**

Comparison of adjectives and adverbs

Whenever you hear **-ší** *shee* or **čí** *tchee* or **ejší** *ayshee* at the end of adjectives, you recognize the comparative degree: dražší *drah-shee* dearer, more expensive; hezčí *hess-chee* prettier, from hezký pretty.

Conjunctions. – Some of them have already been used incidentally:

a	and	když *gdish*	when
ale	but	protože	because
nebo	or	jestli, or: kdyby	if
nejen,	not only,	že	that
ale i...	but also	myslím, že...	I think that...

The general characteristics of Czech

Whereas in English the inflexions (i. e. the changes in the form of words) have been reduced to a minimum,[1] Czech is a highly inflected language.

Case-inflexions (the "endings") have a similar function to prepositions (e. g. of, to, with) and other structural words ˙in English.

The following example gives you an idea of the use of Czech cases. The basic words: syn son; Doktor Novák; matka mother; zpráva report; cesta journey; letadlo aircraft. – Now observe the changes:

Syn	doktor-**a** Novák-**a**	posílá	matc-**e**	zpráv-**u**	**o** cest-**ě**	letadl-**em**
The son	**of** Doctor Novák	sends	to his mother	a report	**on** a journey	**by** plane
1st case Subject	2nd case (Possessive case)	Verb	3rd case Indirect Object	4th case Direct Object	6th case (Prepositional)	7th case (Instrumental)

---

[1] E. g. -ed (he liv-**ed**); -ing (liv-**ing**); -s (he speak-**s**; book-**s**; Dr. Novák**'s** son); -er, -est (small-est); I – **me**, who – who**m**.

Czech prepositions (pp. 30, 34) go with different cases.

NÁPISY	INSCRIPTIONS
ČERSTVĚ NATŘENO	Wet paint
INFORMACE	Informations
PÁNI	Gentlemen
DÁMY	Ladies
MUŽI ŽENY	Men Women
KUŘÁCI	Smokers
KOUŘENÍ ZAKÁZÁNO	No smoking
JED	Poison
LICHÁ (ČÍSLA)	Odd numbers
SUDÁ (ČÍSLA)	Even numbers
NEDOTÝKAT SE!	Don't touch!
NOUZOVÝ VÝCHOD	Emergency Exit
OBSAZENO	Occupied, taken
SEM – TAM	Pull – Push
STANICE	Station
STUDENÝ	Cold
TEPLÝ	Warm
VEN	Out
VCHOD	Entrance
VÝCHOD	Exit
VLEVO – VPRAVO	Left – Right
VOLNO	Free
VSTUP ZAKAZÁN	No entrance

INDEX

First published in 1971 by ORBIS Prague.

© ORBIS Prague

This edition published in 1989 by
COLLETS
Denington Road, Wellingborough
Northants NN8 2QT.

Reprinted 1992

Printed in Great Britain by
Stanley L. Hunt (Printers) Ltd
Midland Road, Rushden, Northants